COUNTRY GREW

TO 1826

CANADA

MAINE
1820

VERMONT
1791

NEW HAMPSHIRE

MASSACHUSETTS
★Boston

NEW YORK

RHODE ISLAND

CONNECTICUT

★New York City

PENNSYLVANIA

NEW
JERSEY

Philadelphia★

MARY-
LAND

DELAWARE

POTOMAC RIVER

★Washington, D.C.

ILLINOIS
1818

INDIANA
1816

OHIO
1803

VIRGINIA
Charlottesville★
Richmond★ ★Yorktown
Williamsburg

MISSOURI
1821

KENTUCKY
1792

NORTH CAROLINA

TENNESSEE
1796

SOUTH CAROLINA

MISSISSIPPI RIVER

MISSISSIPPI
1817

ALABAMA
1819

GEORGIA

LOUISIANA
1812

★New Orleans

BOOK CLUB EDITION

Meet
Thomas Jefferson

By MARVIN BARRETT
Illustrated by ANGELO TORRES

Step-Up Books ⌐_⌐ Random House
New York

To Elizabeth, Irving,
Mary Ellin, and Katherine.

Contents

1
MEET THOMAS JEFFERSON

Thomas Jefferson was the third President of the United States. And he was one of the most important Americans who ever lived.

Jefferson fought for his country. But he did not fight with a gun or a sword. He fought with words.

Thomas Jefferson wrote one of the most famous papers in the world. Many people think it is the greatest paper in American history. It is the Declaration of Independence.

Thomas Jefferson was born in Virginia on April 13, 1743. There was no United States of America then. Virginia was called a colony. It belonged to England. There were 13 colonies in America ruled by the English King.

Virginia was the biggest colony. It went from the sea west to the mountains. The land near the sea was called the Tidewater. It was good farm land. Rich people lived there on great farms. These farms were called plantations.

West of the Tidewater the land grew wilder. In the mountains lived many Indians. But the only white people there were a few hunters.

Thomas Jefferson was born in a house called Shadwell. It was on a farm between the Tidewater and the mountains.

Tom's father was named Peter. He was a farmer. Tom's mother, Jane, came from an old Virginia family named Randolph.

Sometimes Peter Jefferson went west into the mountains. There he visited his friends the Indians. He hunted and explored. He made the first complete map of Virginia.

Sometimes Peter rode east to the Tidewater. There he visited Jane's cousin, William Randolph. Mr. Randolph lived near the sea in a fine house called Tuckahoe.

2
TUCKAHOE

One summer morning when Tom
was only two, the Jefferson family
left Shadwell. Tom, his mother and
father, and his three sisters were
moving to Tuckahoe. Mr. Randolph
had died. Tom's father had promised
to care for the Randolph children.

Tom was too little to ride all by
himself. He had to sit on a pillow
in front of a grownup.

The family rode for three days. At last they came to Tuckahoe.

Tuckahoe was much grander than Shadwell. Ships from England tied up at docks near by. In the ships were beautiful English chairs and fine English china for the house. The ships left filled with tobacco from the Tidewater plantations.

At the big house there were many slaves. Slaves were Negro men and women. They were brought from Africa to work on the plantations.

The slaves were bought and sold like animals. They had to do just what their owners told them. Some owners were cruel. Slavery was one thing Tom Jefferson never liked.

One thing Tom always liked was learning. At Tuckahoe the children had their own little schoolhouse.

There they learned to read, write, and do arithmetic.

Tom did not have any brothers. But one of the Randolph children was a boy about Tom's age. His name was Tom, too. The two Toms became good friends.

Near the schoolhouse was a pond. In the winter the boys skated on it. In the summer they swam in it.

The Jefferson family stayed at Tuckahoe for seven years. By then the Randolph children had grown old enough to care for themselves.

The Jeffersons packed their things. They said good-by and headed home for Shadwell.

3
GROWING UP AT SHADWELL

At Shadwell Tom grew into a big, strong boy. He had freckles and red hair. His nose turned up at the end. His hands and feet were large. He was awkward, but he was a good rider. He and his friends often raced their horses. They went swimming in the river. They went hunting in the woods.

Tom's best friend was a boy named Dabney Carr. Dabney's horse was fast. Tom's was slow. But Tom bet that Dabney could not beat him in a horse race on February 30.

Dabney knew his horse could run faster than Tom's. He said he would be glad to race.

Days went by. February 28 came. Dabney thought he would be racing Tom just two days later.

But the next day was March 1.

All at once Dabney saw that Tom had played a trick. He could not beat Tom on February 30. There was no such day.

Tom had won his bet.

One night an Indian chief came to dinner at Shadwell. His name was Ontasseté. Tom listened to his father and Ontasseté talk. Tom liked the Indians. They were a proud and handsome people.

When Tom was only 14, his father died. Tom was now the head of the family. For a 14-year-old boy he was very rich. He owned a lot of land. He owned 30 slaves. He owned cows and pigs and horses.

Tom was going to a school near Shadwell. He could leave school now if he wanted to. He had no father to tell him what to do.

But Tom stayed in school. There he learned two more languages, Greek and Latin. And on his own, he learned to play the violin.

When Tom was 16, he decided to go to college. He packed his bags. He rode off to Williamsburg, the capital of Virginia.

4
TOM GOES TO COLLEGE

Williamsburg was the biggest town Tom had ever seen. There were 300 houses. The main street was 100 feet wide. It was covered with sand and oyster shells. At one end of it stood the Capitol Building.

There, men from all over Virginia came to make laws. These men were called burgesses. And together they were called the House of Burgesses.

From the Capitol, Tom rode down the main street of Williamsburg. At the far end stood some low brick buildings. This was the College of William and Mary.

At William and Mary, Tom studied hard. Most of the other boys played cards and raced their horses. They kept slaves and spent their money on fine clothes. Tom had fun, but his studies came first.

One night one of Tom's teachers took him to the finest house in Williamsburg. It was the governor's house. The governor had come from England. He had been sent by the King to run Virginia.

The governor liked young Thomas Jefferson. Tom came back often. He learned a lot from the governor and his friends. Tom knew that he could learn from people as well as books.

One day a large band of Indians came to Williamsburg. Their chief was Peter Jefferson's old friend Ontasseté. He was going to England to meet King George the Third.

That night Ontasseté made a good-by speech. There was a full moon. The Indians sat very still. Their chief's voice was strong and clear.

It was a night Tom remembered all his life.

5
BECOMING A LAWYER

When Tom finished college, he decided to be a lawyer. In those days a man could become a lawyer in six weeks. Tom wanted to be the best lawyer in Virginia. He worked for five years.

He got up every morning at five o'clock. To wake himself up he put his feet in cold water. At night he studied long past midnight. He felt a good lawyer should know other things besides law. So Tom studied history and science and geography. He learned to read and write in six languages.

Tom did not work all the time. For fun he played his violin. He danced with the girls in Williamsburg. He often went riding. And there was good swimming in a pond near by.

Tom made many friends. One of his best friends was a man named Patrick Henry. Henry was a poor man. But he was a lawyer and a burgess. He and Tom talked about many things. One thing they were both worried about was taxes. They thought King George was making Americans pay too many taxes.

There were taxes on all kinds of things, like food and iron and rum. Every piece of paper a lawyer used had to have a tax stamp on it.

One day Henry stood up in the House of Burgesses. He spoke out against King George. He called the King a tyrant. A tyrant is a cruel ruler. He said other tyrants had been killed.

Many burgesses did not like what he said. They were afraid the King would be very angry. But Jefferson thought his friend was right. He, too, thought the King was a tyrant.

Henry's words were printed in the newspapers. They were read in all the colonies. Many other people thought Patrick Henry was right.

6
MONTICELLO

Jefferson became a lawyer in 1767. He was a country lawyer. He rode for miles through the hills around Shadwell. He helped many people. Many of them were poor. He never asked the poor people to pay him.

When he was 25, Tom Jefferson decided he wanted to be a burgess. He had many friends in the country around Shadwell. They all voted for him. He won the election.

He was one of the youngest men in the House of Burgesses.

Jefferson went to Williamsburg. There he met the other burgesses. One was a rich farmer and famous soldier named George Washington.

The burgesses sent a letter to the King. They wanted England to stop taxing America. They said that the colonies wanted to make their own laws and taxes.

King George told the governor to dissolve the House of Burgesses. This meant that new burgesses had to be elected.

The people elected the same men all over again.

Jefferson was very busy. He was still working as a lawyer. And he was building a new house.

Jefferson's new house would be on a hill near Shadwell. He called it Monticello. He wanted to make it the finest house in the colonies. He planned all sorts of new things for his house.

It would have doors that opened all by themselves. There would be little elevators to carry food from one floor to the next. He drew plans for a big clock to stand in the hall. It would run for seven days without winding. Also in the hall would be an arrow. It would show which way the wind blew outside.

One day a slave came to him with bad news. Shadwell had burned to the ground.

Now Jefferson worked harder than ever on Monticello. In a few months a small part of the house was done. Jefferson moved in.

Around the house he planted many flowers and fruit trees. There were oranges, apples, pears, figs, and nuts. Many of the things he grew had never been seen in Virginia before.

By now Jefferson was not working on Monticello just for himself. He had met a beautiful woman named Martha Skelton. He had fallen in love with her.

Jefferson was not the only one to fall in love with Martha. There were many other young men who wanted to marry her. For she was not only pretty. She was smart and lively.

Martha and Tom both loved music. One night they were playing together at Martha's house. Other young men came to call. They stood on the door-step. They could hear the music coming from inside.

The young men knew Jefferson had won her. They went away.

7
A WIFE AND A WAR

Tom and Martha were married on New Year's Day, 1772. They went to live at Monticello.

In the fall Martha had a baby girl. She was called Patsy. The Jefferson family needed more room now. Tom and his men worked hard to finish Monticello.

The Jeffersons were very happy. But soon Tom had to leave home. He was needed in Williamsburg.

Virginia had a new governor. His name was Lord Dunmore. He did not like the House of Burgesses at all. He dissolved the House again and again. But he could not keep the burgesses from meeting.

In March of 1773 they met in a place called the Raleigh Tavern. There they picked 11 men. One was Patrick Henry. And one was Thomas Jefferson.

These men were to write letters to the other colonies. They wanted to find out what other men were doing about the English laws and taxes. Many letters went back and forth. The colonies were drawing together against England.

In November of 1773 three ships from England came into the harbor of Boston, Massachusetts. They were loaded with tea.

On the night of December 16 some men dressed up as Indians. They went onto the ships. They dumped all the tea into the water.

They thought it was a good joke. They said it was a tea party for King George. They called it the Boston Tea Party.

King George did not think it was funny. He closed Boston Harbor. He said no more ships could go there. He sent more soldiers to America.

In March, 1775, Jefferson sat in a church in Richmond, Virginia. His friend Patrick Henry was giving a speech. He was asking Americans to fight the King. "Give me liberty or give me death!" he cried.

News of his words raced like wind across the land. In all 13 colonies men shouted, "Liberty or death!"

In Massachusetts, farmers fired on English soldiers. Men on both sides were killed.

This was the beginning of a war between England and its colonies.

It was the American Revolution.

The leaders of the colonies met in the city of Philadelphia. They called the meeting the Continental Congress.

Jefferson set out for Philadelphia.

The Continental Congress had many problems. Most important was to find a general for the army. The Congress chose George Washington.

In the late summer Jefferson went home to Monticello. It was not a happy time. A baby daughter died. A few months later his mother died. And his wife was sick. Jefferson stayed as long as he could. But in May of 1776 he had to go back to Philadelphia.

8
THE DECLARATION
OF INDEPENDENCE

All through the hot summer of 1776 Jefferson went to meetings of the Continental Congress. There were many things to do. They had to have a bigger army. They had to have a navy. And they had to raise the money to run them both.

The fighting had been going on for a year. The congressmen decided it was time to tell the world what the Americans were fighting for.

They chose five men to write down the reasons.

One of the men was John Adams. He later became a President of the United States. One was Benjamin Franklin. He was one of the most famous men in America. And one was Thomas Jefferson.

Jefferson was the youngest of the men. But they had all read papers he had written. They all agreed he was the best man for the job.

Jefferson went to work. His room was small and stuffy. Horse flies buzzed around his head. They bit. The days were long and hot.

It took 18 days to write the paper.

It was only one page.

But Thomas Jefferson had written the Declaration of Independence.

The Declaration of Independence said that all men had certain rights. They had the right to be free. They had the right to choose their own rulers. If a ruler was bad, they had the right to choose another. Americans had decided that King George of England was a bad ruler.

The Declaration said the colonies were not English any more. They were now the 13 "united States of America."

9
NEW LAWS FOR A NEW STATE

The other men in Congress read
the Declaration. They talked about
it. They changed a few words. Then
on July 4, 1776, they agreed to sign
it. Copies were made. One copy was
read to Washington's soldiers in
Massachusetts. They cheered.

In Philadelphia a big crowd heard
it read. They cheered, too. All over
America people rang bells. They
fired off guns. They lit up the sky
with bonfires and fireworks.

In September Jefferson rode home
to Virginia.

The new governor of Virginia was
an American. He was Patrick Henry.
The burgesses were called delegates
now. Jefferson took his seat in the
House of Delegates in Williamsburg.

Virginia was no longer a colony. It was now the biggest and richest state in the new country. Jefferson hoped that if it made good laws the other states would copy them.

Washington was leading America in the war against the English King. Jefferson wanted to lead the fight against the old English laws.

Many of the laws were cruel. One said a woman could be burned as a witch. Another said a man could be hanged for stealing. Jefferson worked hard to change these laws.

Slaves were sent to Virginia on ships and sold. Jefferson could not stop slavery. But he stopped the slave ships from coming to Virginia.

Another of his laws set up free schools for poor children. Still another was about religion.

All Virginians had to pay money to the Church of England. Even the people who went to other churches had to pay. Jefferson wanted to stop this. But most delegates belonged to the Church of England. They did not pass his law.

To Jefferson the new country was like an empty notebook. He wanted to help put the right words in it.

In 1778 Martha had another baby. The Jeffersons called her Polly.

That same year the King of France sent soldiers to help the Americans fight the English.

The French soldiers were led by the Marquis de Lafayette. Lafayette was only 19. But he was already a general. He and Jefferson became great friends.

In 1779 Jefferson became governor of Virginia.

Virginia was lucky. Up to now no battles had been fought there. Most of the fighting was in the North. Governor Jefferson sent soldiers north to help General Washington. He sent him food and money, guns and horses. Then, in 1781, English warships sailed up the rivers of Virginia. English soldiers landed. The Virginians tried to fight back. But there were not enough soldiers.

Most of them were up north. The English pressed on into Virginia.

Soon Jefferson had to move the state capital west to Richmond. In a short time the capital was moved west again, to Charlottesville.

Jefferson stayed on at Monticello. One morning an American captain rode up the hill. He told Jefferson that English soldiers were coming to get him.

10
AMERICA WINS THE WAR

The Jefferson family was having breakfast with some friends. The friends left. Jefferson sent Martha and the girls away in a carriage.

Soon a man ran to him. English soldiers were climbing the hill! The man begged Jefferson to go.

Jefferson let himself out by the back door. He jumped on his horse. He galloped down the hill.

He did not ride along the roads. He kept to the woods. The English soldiers could not find him. When night fell, he and his family were safe at a friend's house.

In October, 1781, there was a great battle at Yorktown, Virginia. 8,000 English soldiers were trapped. On the sea behind them were French warships. On the land before them were American and French armies.

The American general was George Washington. The French general was the Marquis de Lafayette.

American and French cannonballs battered the English for two weeks. One night the English tried to get away in boats. A bad storm came up. It drove the boats back to land. The next morning the English gave up.

Yorktown was the last big battle of the Revolution. The Americans had won the war.

Jefferson was not the governor of Virginia any more. His two years as head of the state had been hard. He was glad that his country was at peace. Now he hoped he could live in peace at Monticello.

In 1782 Jefferson was elected a delegate again. But he would not leave home. He wanted to be with his family. Martha was very sick. All spring and summer he was at her bedside.

September 6, 1782 was the worst day of Jefferson's life. He wrote a few sad words in a book. "My dear wife died this day at 11:45 A.M."

11
NEW IDEAS FOR A
NEW COUNTRY

When Martha died, Jefferson was heartbroken. He shut himself in his room. He did not eat or speak for days. For three long weeks little Patsy brought him food. She took care of him. She did all she could to cheer him up.

At last he came out. He saddled his favorite horse. He rode out alone across the hills.

His friends felt that he should go back to work. The Continental Congress was meeting. His friends asked him to go. Once more he set off for Philadelphia.

In Congress no one could agree on anything. Everyone talked. No one listened. No one wanted to give any money to run the new country. They did not even know what kind of government they wanted.

America owned land west of the 13 states. Many congressmen wanted the states to divide this land up. It looked as though the 13 states might become 13 little countries.

Jefferson said that the western lands should become new states.

The congressmen agreed with his plan. But they would not agree to keep slavery out of the new lands.

Jefferson also said that America needed its own money. He invented a new kind of money. It was made up of dollars worth 100 cents each. It was the simplest money in the world. Again Congress agreed.

In 1784 Congress asked him to go to France. France had been a good friend during the war. Both John Adams and Benjamin Franklin were there. Jefferson could help them make new friends for America in other countries in Europe.

He decided to leave Polly with an aunt and take Patsy with him.

12
FRANCE

On July 4 Jefferson and Patsy arrived in Boston. A ship called the Ceres was waiting there. They went on board. The next morning they were off to France.

Jefferson found that France was in trouble. The French King and the people in his government were very rich. But most of the people in the country were very poor. And the King was not helping them.

Jefferson went all over Europe. Everywhere he went he looked for new things to send home. He sent plants and trees. He sent animals and birds. And he sent books. He sent 200 books to a young friend of his named James Madison.

Madison was in Virginia. He was working to get the delegates to pass the laws that Jefferson had written long before.

At last the delegates agreed to pass Jefferson's laws about religion. These laws did away with religious taxes. They said everyone could worship God in his own way. The laws were called the Statute of Virginia for Religious Freedom.

Jefferson often wrote to another young friend. His name was James Monroe. He was working with James Madison on the Constitution of the United States. The Constitution set up a new government for America. Even though Jefferson was far away they wanted his help.

Jefferson's French friends wanted his help, too. Many thought the new American government was the best in the world. Lafayette thought the French government should copy it.

On July 4, 1789, Jefferson gave a party. Lafayette was there. It was a happy night. They had worked out a new plan. It would give the French people many more rights.

But it was too late.

On July 14 thousands of people marched on the King's prison. They let the prisoners out. They cut off the prison keepers' heads.

Jefferson saw the people running through the city streets. He saw them throwing rocks at the King's soldiers. He saw them breaking into stores to get knives and swords.

A revolution had begun.

Jefferson had spent five years in France. Now he had to go back to America.

In September the Jeffersons were waiting for the ship to take them home. A man brought them news. The King and Queen of France had been taken prisoner. The people of France said they were tyrants.

All wars are terrible. The French Revolution was one of the worst. Thousands of people were killed. And when it was over, France had a new tyrant. His name was Napoleon.

The Jeffersons were lucky they could leave France when they did.

13
AMERICANS CHOOSE SIDES

Two days before Christmas, 1789, Jefferson's coach rolled to a stop in front of Monticello. His slaves ran to him. Laughing and crying, they carried him into the house.

Not long after Christmas, a young man began to call at Monticello. He came to see Patsy. His name was Thomas Mann Randolph. He was the son of Jefferson's boyhood friend, Tom Randolph of Tuckahoe.

In February, 1790, Patsy married Thomas. In March Jefferson left home again. He went to the capital of America, New York City.

George Washington was now the President of the United States. He had asked Jefferson to be Secretary of State. Jefferson would take care of business with other countries.

Jefferson did many other things. He ran the mint where the money was made. He ran the office where new inventions were brought.

Like these inventions, everything in the new country had to be tested. People did not always agree on the way things should be done.

The men who helped Washington run the country chose up sides. Some men followed Jefferson. They were called Democrat-Republicans. Other men were called Federalists.

They were led by the Secretary of the Treasury, Alexander Hamilton.

Hamilton had been a poor boy. But his side was for the rich. It was for people in big cities. It was for people in the North.

Jefferson was rich. But his side was for the poor. He was the friend of farmers and people in the South and the West.

Both men worked very hard for their country. But they had many arguments.

Hamilton wanted the new capital of the country to be in the North. Jefferson wanted it farther south, on the Potomac River. The river divides Maryland and Virginia.

61

Jefferson won the argument.

Maryland and Virginia gave some land to the government. The new city would be named Washington, after the first President.

In 1797 Thomas Jefferson ran for President against Federalist John Adams. John Adams won. Jefferson became Vice President.

President Adams signed many new laws. Jefferson felt many of them were very bad. One said that people from other countries had to wait 14 years to become Americans.

The worst laws kept people from speaking out against the American government. People from Europe could be sent back home. Americans could be sent to jail.

Jefferson could do nothing to help these people. Americans had fought a long war to win their rights. Now Jefferson was afraid these rights were being taken away.

There were many other Americans who agreed with Jefferson. In 1801 they voted against Adams. Thomas Jefferson was elected President of the United States.

John Adams was very angry. He left Washington without waiting to see Jefferson become President.

14

PRESIDENT JEFFERSON

On March 4, 1801, Jefferson set out from his room in the new city of Washington. He did not ride in a carriage. He walked. The path ran through a swamp. His shoes were covered with mud when he got to the Capitol Building.

There, Jefferson swore to uphold the laws of the country. He was now the third President of the United States.

Jefferson was not at all like the other Presidents. He did not like big parties. He did not like fancy clothes. People who came to see him often found him playing with his grandchildren on the floor.

Some people did not think that a President should be so easy-going.

Once the English ambassador, a very important man, came to call. Jefferson met him wearing an old suit and slippers. The ambassador was very angry. He thought that the American President should dress up to meet him.

But most Americans thought that Jefferson was right. They liked his easy ways.

President Jefferson had bigger things to worry him. In the north of Africa there were a lot of pirates called the Tripoli pirates. America was paying them to leave American ships alone. Now the pirates were asking for more money.

Jefferson grew angry. He moved fast. He did not send the money. He sent warships to fight the pirates.

Jefferson knew America had to fight. But he did not like wars. He thought the most important thing was learning. And there was still much to learn about America.

The West of America was still wild. Jefferson wanted to learn about it.

15
THE LOUISIANA PURCHASE

The United States went as far as the Mississippi River. No one knew much about the wild land beyond.

Jefferson's secretary was a man named Meriwether Lewis. Jefferson chose him to explore the Far West. Lewis called in an old friend named William Clark to go with him.

Jefferson told them he wanted to know about the mountains and the rivers in that part of America. He wanted to know about the Indians there. He wanted to know about the animals and birds and plants.

A year later, Lewis and Clark left.

France owned a huge part of the West. The French land lay between the Mississippi River and the Rocky Mountains. It was called Louisiana. The capital of Louisiana was the city of New Orleans.

New Orleans was very important to American farmers in the West. They sent cotton and other crops down the Mississippi River to New Orleans. There the crops were sold. Then ships carried them to cities in America and other countries.

The French could close up New Orleans at any time. Ships would not be able to come or go. American farmers would have nowhere to sell their crops. They would be ruined.

President Jefferson knew he had to do something. He sent his friend James Monroe to France. He told Monroe to try to buy New Orleans.

Napoleon, the head of the French government, said no. He would not sell New Orleans by itself. But he would sell all of Louisiana for 25 million dollars.

Monroe said America could not pay that much. The talks went on. At last Napoleon sold Louisiana for 15 million dollars.

Napoleon fought wars to get more land. Thousands of men died in his wars. With the Louisiana Purchase Jefferson made America twice as big. And not a man was killed.

16
PRESIDENT AGAIN

As President, things were going well for Thomas Jefferson. But he was worried about his family. Polly was very sick.

Polly was staying with her sister Patsy. Jefferson decided to take her to Monticello.

There he spent as much time as he could with her. He read to her. He took her on rides around the garden. A slave pulled the little carriage along slowly so it would not bump too much.

But in April, 1804, Polly died. Her father was heartbroken.

Far away in Massachusetts, John Adams's wife heard the sad news. She wrote Jefferson a kind note. It was the first time he had heard from her since he became President. He wrote a note back. Soon he and the Adamses were friends again.

In the fall of 1804, Jefferson ran for President again. He was elected for another four years.

In 1805 the war with the Tripoli pirates ended. America won. Never again would America pay the Tripoli pirates to leave its ships alone.

A year later, Meriwether Lewis and William Clark came back from the West. They had gone all the way to the far Pacific Ocean.

It had been a hard trip. They had been gone so long people thought they might be dead. But they had done what Jefferson had hoped they would do.

They brought back Indians with them. They brought back maps of the rivers and mountains. They had books filled with notes about the animals and birds and plants. They even brought back some live grizzly bears. Jefferson kept them in his garden in Washington.

In 1808 many Americans hoped Jefferson would run for President again. But he had worked for his country for 40 years. He wanted to go home to Monticello for good.

17
THE UNIVERSITY OF VIRGINIA

Even at Monticello Jefferson did not stop working. He was up early every morning. He rode, he farmed, and he studied. He read to his 12 grandchildren and played with them. He made them a fruit-picker. It was a hook on the end of a long stick. There was a bag on it to catch the apples and oranges as they fell. Even a very small child could get fruit from the trees with it.

Thomas Jefferson was now called the sage of Monticello. A sage is a wise man. He is almost always an old man who has lived a long and useful life. He has done and seen many things. He has been happy and sad. He knows what life is about.

People were always asking Thomas Jefferson for advice. He got over 1,000 letters every year. His friend James Madison wrote to him. He was the fourth President of the United States. So did James Monroe, the fifth President. They still thought of Jefferson as their teacher.

The man who wrote most often was John Adams. They were the closest of friends until the day they died.

In 1820 Jefferson was 77. But he was busier than ever. Early most mornings he would ride four miles over to Charlottesville. There he was building a college. It was to be the University of Virginia.

Jefferson spent six years working on the University. His old friends President Madison and President Monroe helped him. But he did most of the work himself.

He made plans of the buildings and the gardens. He told the builders how much brick and stone and wood was needed. He sent men all the way to Europe to find good teachers. He wanted the University to be the best in America.

Slowly the college buildings grew. Sometimes he could not go over to Charlottesville. Then he went out on his porch and watched the work through a telescope.

At last the college was finished. Jefferson made friends with many of the students. He would ask them up to Monticello for dinner.

There were always people coming to Monticello. It was like a hotel. There were 50 beds for people who wanted to stay for the night. One family stayed for ten months.

Everyone wanted to see Jefferson.

80

Even people he did not know would come into his house. They would wait for hours just to see the great man walk down the hall to dinner. One lady broke a window with her parasol to get a look at him.

Monticello cost a lot of money to run. Jefferson was not rich any more. He sold his 10,000 books to Congress. They were the beginning of the great Library of Congress.

But this money did not last long. For a while it looked as if he would have to sell Monticello.

People all over the country heard of his troubles. They began to send money to help Jefferson. They saved Monticello for him.

18
THE LAST DAYS

One day a carriage rolled up to Monticello. Out stepped an old man. He moved slowly toward the house. Jefferson came out to meet him.

"Ah, Jefferson!" the visitor cried.

"Ah, Lafayette!" cried Jefferson. And they both burst into tears.

It was a happy visit. The two old friends had not seen each other for 36 years. They had many things to talk about.

They talked about the American and the French Revolutions. They talked about all the people they had known. They talked of the past and the future. They were old men now. And they had each played a big part in the history of their countries.

July 4, 1826 was a big holiday in America. It was just 50 years since Thomas Jefferson had written the Declaration of Independence. Two of the most famous men who signed it were still alive. They were John Adams and Thomas Jefferson. John Adams was 91. Jefferson was 83.

At Monticello Jefferson lay in bed. He knew he was dying. But he had fought to stay alive until this day.

It was a great day. All over the country guns were fired. Soldiers marched. Flags waved in the wind.

At Monticello it was quiet. Soon after noon, Thomas Jefferson died. Later on the same day, far away in Massachusetts, John Adams died.

It is hard to say what was most important in Jefferson's life. He did many things. He doubled the size of his country without a war. He gave it many good laws. He was one of its greatest leaders. And he was a teacher to the Presidents who followed him.

After Thomas Jefferson died, an old book was found in his desk. On one page was a drawing.

The drawing was of his tombstone.
Jefferson had written the words he
wanted on it.

"Here was buried
Thomas Jefferson
Author of the
Declaration of American
Independence
of the Statute of Virginia
for religious freedom
and Father of
the University of Virginia."

"By these," he had written, "I
wish most to be remembered."

THE WAY THE
FROM THE REVOLUTION

THE LOUISIANA PURCHASE

MEXICO

The United States from the American Revolution to 1826

 These were the first 13 states in the United States.

 These had become states by the time Thomas Jefferson died in 1826. The dates show the years they became states.

 The Louisiana Purchase.

 Important places in the life of Thomas Jefferson.